SUPER
SIMPLE
ORIGAMI

ORIGAMI
DINOSAURS

Easy & Fun Paper-Folding Projects

Anna George

Consulting Editor, Diane Craig, M.A./Reading Specialist

Super Sandcastle

An Imprint of Abdo Publishing
abdopublishing.com

abdopublishing.com

Published by Abdo Publishing, a division of ABDO, PO Box 398166, Minneapolis, Minnesota 55439.
Copyright © 2017 by Abdo Consulting Group, Inc. International copyrights reserved in all countries.
No part of this book may be reproduced in any form without written permission from the publisher.
Super SandCastle™ is a trademark and logo of Abdo Publishing.

Printed in the United States of America, North Mankato, Minnesota
102016
012017

Editor: Liz Salzmann
Content Developer: Nancy Tuminelly
Cover and Interior Design and Production: Mighty Media, Inc.
Photo Credits: iStockphoto; Mighty Media, Inc.
Special Thanks to Kazuko Collins

The following manufacturers/names appearing in this book are trademarks: Elmer's® Glue-All®

Publisher's Cataloging-in-Publication Data
Names: George, Anna, author.
Title: Origami dinosaurs: easy & fun paper-folding projects / by Anna George.
Other titles: Easy & fun paper-folding projects | Easy and fun paper-folding projects
Description: Minneapolis, MN : Abdo Publishing, 2017. | Series: Super simple origami
Identifiers: LCCN 2016944709 | ISBN 9781680784473 (lib. bdg.) |
    ISBN 9781680798005 (ebook)
Subjects: LCSH: Dinosaurs in art--Juvenile literature. | Origami--Juvenile
    Literature. | Paper work--Juvenile literature. | Handicraft--Juvenile literature.
Classification: DDC 736/.982--dc23
LC record available at http://lccn.loc.gov/2016944709

Super SandCastle™ books are created by a team of professional educators, reading specialists, and content developers around five essential components—phonemic awareness, phonics, vocabulary, text comprehension, and fluency—to assist young readers as they develop reading skills and strategies and increase their general knowledge. All books are written, reviewed, and leveled for guided reading and early reading intervention programs for use in shared, guided, and independent reading and writing activities to support a balanced approach to literacy instruction.

CONTENTS

AMAZING ORIGAMI DINOSAURS

Origami is the art of folding paper. In Japanese, the word *ori* means "to fold" and *gami* means "paper." People in Japan and all around the world enjoy origami.

Do you have a favorite dinosaur? Is it a *T. rex*? Or maybe an *Allosaurus*? This book will show you how to make those dinosaurs and more! These super simple origami projects are great for beginners. You will learn about:

- different types of paper folds
- **symbols** used in origami **diagrams**
- types of paper that will work for origami

You'll be **amazed** at what you can make with just one sheet of paper!

BASIC FOLDS

MOUNTAIN FOLD
Fold behind to create a mountain.

VALLEY FOLD
Fold in front to create a valley.

CREASE
Fold and unfold to make a **crease**.

ORIGAMI SYMBOLS

The **symbols** below show the most common actions used in origami.

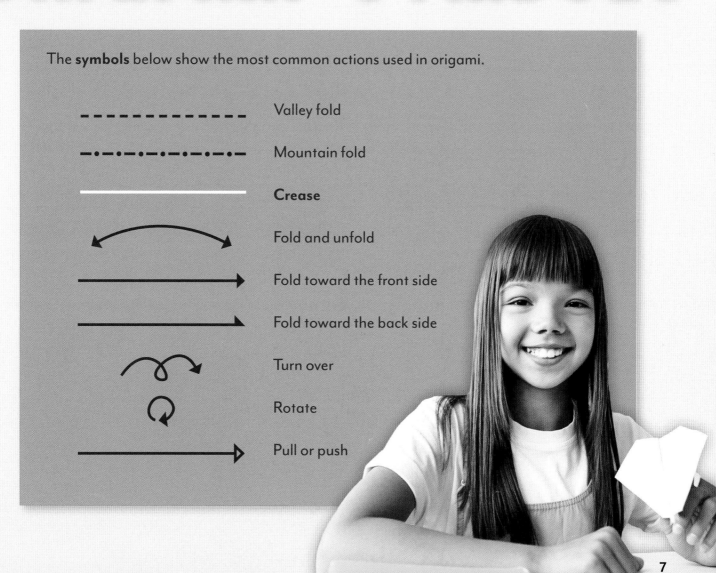

- - - - - - - - - - - Valley fold

- · - · - · - · - · - · Mountain fold

—————————— **Crease**

Fold and unfold

Fold toward the front side

Fold toward the back side

Turn over

Rotate

Pull or push

SPECIAL FOLDS

INSIDE REVERSE FOLD

This fold is often used to make the head or feet of an animal.
It may seem hard at first. After you practice it will become easier.
Here are instructions to make this fold.

1

Fold a square piece of
paper into a triangle. Valley
fold one of the points.

2

Crease it firmly.
Unfold.

3

Mountain fold the
crease. Unfold.

4

Unfold the paper. Place it so the
center crease is vertical. Valley
fold the bottom point.

5

Refold the
center crease.

OUTSIDE REVERSE FOLD

This fold is often used to make the head of a bird or the feet of an animal. It is just like the inside **reverse** fold except the corner is folded on the outside.

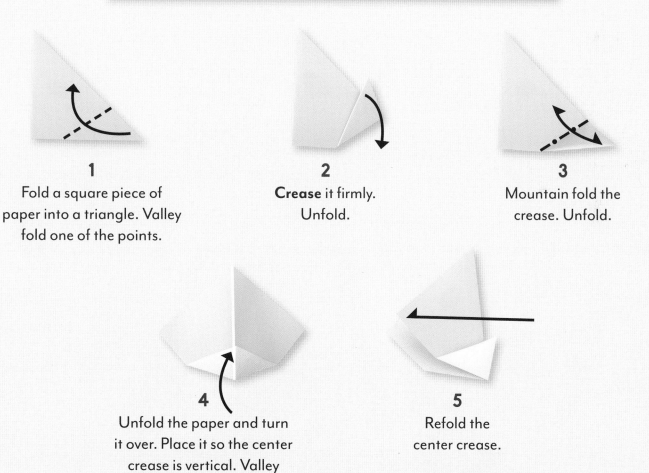

1
Fold a square piece of paper into a triangle. Valley fold one of the points.

2
Crease it firmly. Unfold.

3
Mountain fold the crease. Unfold.

4
Unfold the paper and turn it over. Place it so the center crease is vertical. Valley fold the bottom point.

5
Refold the center crease.

BASES

These shapes are used as bases for many different origami models. Practicing these will help you improve your origami.

SQUARE BASE

1

Place the paper on the table with a straight edge at the top. Mountain fold the top to the bottom. Unfold.

2

Mountain fold the right side to the left side. Unfold.

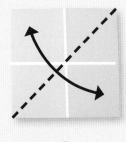

3

Valley fold one point to the opposite point. Unfold.

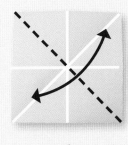

4

Valley fold the other two points together. Unfold.

5

Pinch and lift two opposite mountain folds.

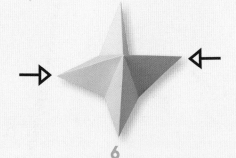

6

Press the sides together.

7

Flatten the paper into a square.

KITE BASE | # BIRD BASE

1

Place a square piece of paper with one point at the top.

2

Valley fold the left point to the right point. Unfold.

3

Valley fold the two side points to the center **crease**.

4

This is the finished kite base.

1

Start with a square base. Place it with the open point at the bottom.

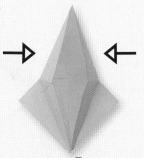

2

Valley fold the top layer of the right point to the center crease.

3

Valley fold the top layer of the left point to the center crease.

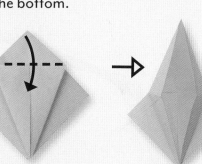

4

Valley fold the top point down. Unfold the last three folds.

5

Lift the top layer of the bottom point. Push the sides together. Flatten the sides.

6

Turn the model over from side to side. Repeat steps 2 through 5.

MATERIALS

BONE FOLDER

CRAFT STICK

PAPER

You can use almost any type of paper for origami. You can get special origami paper at craft stores or online. You can also use copy paper, magazine pages, scrapbooking paper, and even gift wrap!

CREASING TOOLS

The edge of a ruler, craft stick, or bone folder can help you make good **creases** and folds.

SCISSORS

You will need scissors if you are starting with a sheet of paper that isn't square. (See page 13.)

EXTRAS

These are **optional** supplies used in this book.

- googly eyes
- glue
- markers

TIPS AND TRICKS

GET SQUARE

Many origami models use a square piece of paper.
It is easy to make a rectangular piece of paper square.

1 Fold one short edge so it lines up with a long edge. **Crease** the fold.

2 Cut off the strip under the triangle.

3 Unfold the paper. Now you have a square!

PRACTICE MAKES PERFECT!

When folding origami models, it is important for the folds to be as **accurate** as possible. Match up the edges and corners when folding. Make firm creases. The more folds there are, the more important it is to make them exact. So get out some scrap paper and practice, practice, practice!

ALLOSAURUS HEAD

- paper (square)
- marker
- googly eyes
- glue

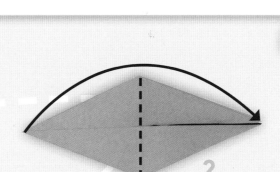

1

Start with a bird base. (See pages 10 and 11.) Place it with the divided point on the right.

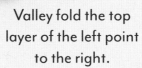

2

Valley fold the top layer of the left point to the right.

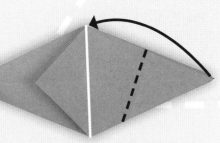

3

Valley fold the same point back to the top of the center **crease**.

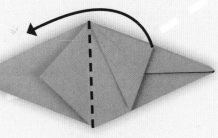

4

Valley fold the top layer on the center crease.

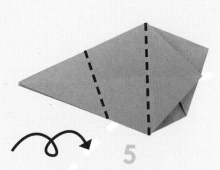

5

Turn the model over from side to side. Valley fold the right point to the left. Then repeat steps 3 and 4.

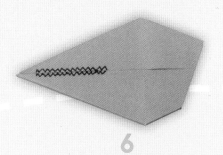

6

Draw teeth along the edges of the divided point on both sides. This is the dinosaur's mouth.

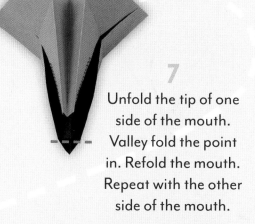

7

Unfold the tip of one side of the mouth. Valley fold the point in. Refold the mouth. Repeat with the other side of the mouth.

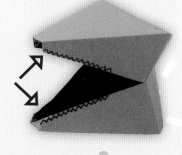

8

Gently pull the back flaps apart. Open up the top and bottom parts of the head by pushing on the inside of the mouth.

9

Mountain fold the tops of the back flaps. Then valley fold the bottoms of the flaps. This keeps them tucked behind the head.

10

Glue a googly eye to each side of the head.

TOWERING
T. REX

• paper (square)
• googly eyes
• glue

1

Start with a kite base.
(See page 11.) Your *T. rex*
will be the color of the
inside. Place the base
with the long point down.

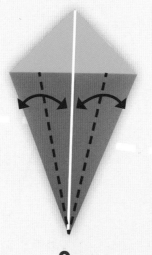

2

Valley fold both
sides to the
center **crease.**
Unfold all the
folds.

3

Mountain fold the
crease to the right
of the center crease.
Unfold.

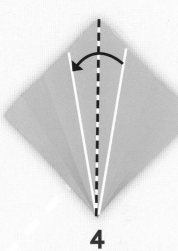

4

Pinch the **crease** you made in step 3. Press it along the crease to the left of the center crease.

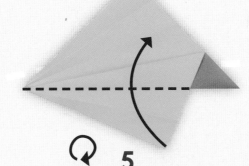

5

Rotate the model to the right. Valley fold the crease that is along the center fold.

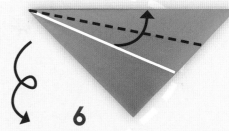

6

Turn the model over from top to bottom. Pinch the second crease from the bottom. Press it along the center fold.

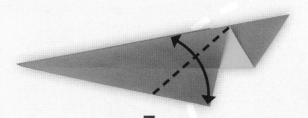

7

Valley fold the bottom point to the center fold. Unfold.

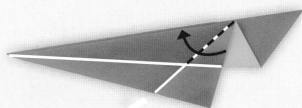

8

Refold the crease you made in step 7. But just fold it between the center fold and the bottom crease.

Continued on the next page.

9

Valley fold the bottom crease from the left point to the **crease** you made in step 7. This will create a triangular flap in the middle.

10

Flatten the flap to the right.

11

Valley fold the flap up so the point is above the center fold. Turn the model over from side to side. Repeat steps 7 through 11 on the opposite side.

12

Rotate the model so the flaps point down. Unfold the top layer.

13

Valley fold the right point slightly above the top point. Unfold.

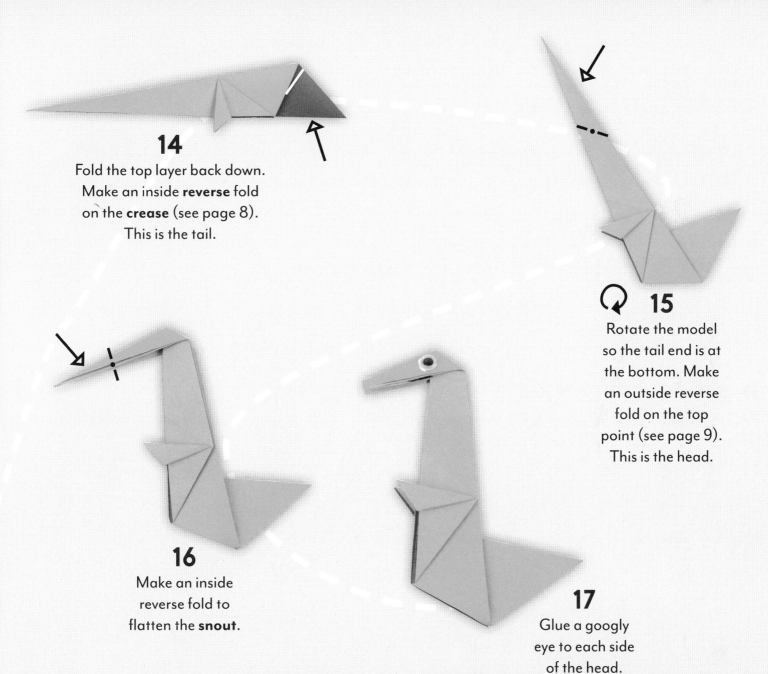

14

Fold the top layer back down.
Make an inside **reverse** fold
on the **crease** (see page 8).
This is the tail.

15

Rotate the model
so the tail end is at
the bottom. Make
an outside reverse
fold on the top
point (see page 9).
This is the head.

16

Make an inside
reverse fold to
flatten the **snout**.

17

Glue a googly
eye to each side
of the head.

BRAVE BRACHIOSAURUS

- paper (square)
- googly eyes
- glue

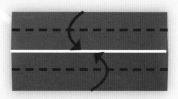

1

Place the paper on the table with a straight edge at the top.

2

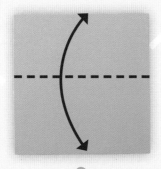

Valley fold the bottom to the top. Unfold.

3

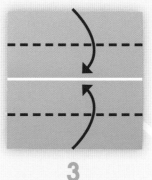

Valley fold the top and bottom edges to the center **crease**.

4

Valley fold the top and bottom edges to the center crease again.

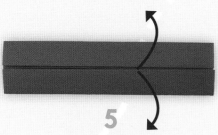

5

Unfold the
folds you made
in step 4.

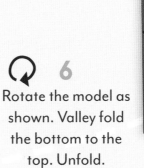

6

Rotate the model as
shown. Valley fold
the bottom to the
top. Unfold.

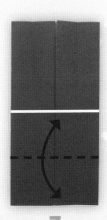

7

Valley fold the
bottom edge
to the center
crease. Unfold.

8

Valley fold both
bottom points
to the bottom
crease. Unfold.

Continued
on the
next page.

9

Lift the corner of the right side of the top layer. Pull it up to the center **crease**. Flatten it into a triangle. Repeat on the left side.

10

Valley fold both flaps to the bottom point.

11

Mountain fold the right side to the left side.

12

Valley fold the top layer of the point to the bottom crease. Turn the model over from side to side. Valley fold the other layer the same way.

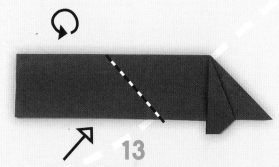

13

Rotate the model so the point is on the right. Valley fold the left side up. Make an inside **reverse** fold on the crease (see page 8).

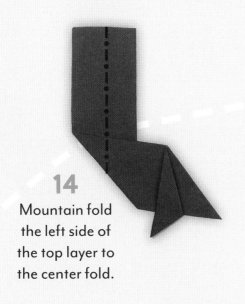

14
Mountain fold the left side of the top layer to the center fold.

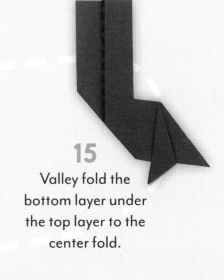

15
Valley fold the bottom layer under the top layer to the center fold.

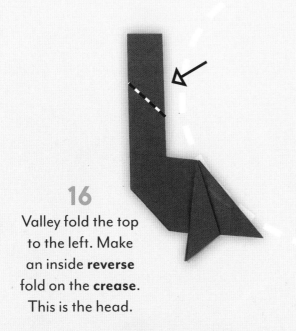

16
Valley fold the top to the left. Make an inside **reverse** fold on the **crease**. This is the head.

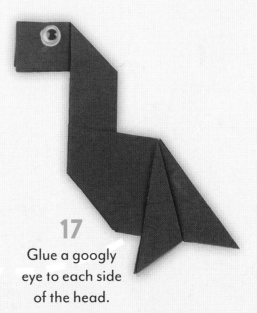

17
Glue a googly eye to each side of the head.

PLESIOSAURUS PAL

- paper (square)
- googly eyes
- glue

1

Start with a kite base. (See page 11.) Your dinosaur will be the color of the inside. Place the base with the long point down.

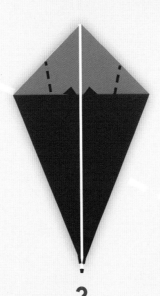

2

Valley fold the sides to the center **crease**. Unfold.

3

Valley fold each side of the top layer from the center to the **outer** folds.

4

Valley fold the right point to the left point. Rotate the model so the center fold is on the bottom.

5

Valley fold the top two layers to the center fold.

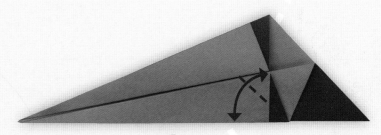

6

Valley fold the corner of the top flap to the bottom edge. Unfold.

Continued on the next page.

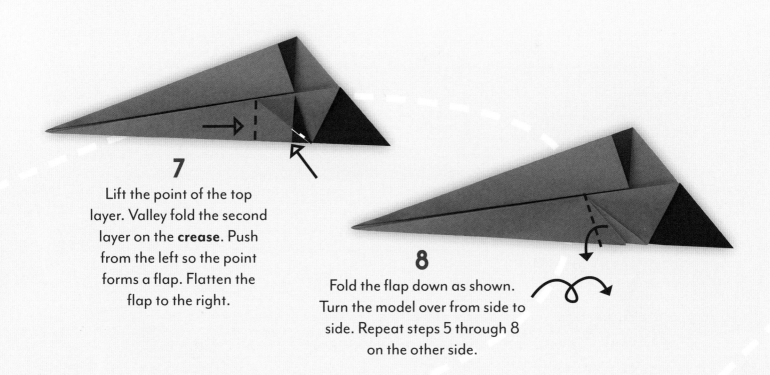

7

Lift the point of the top layer. Valley fold the second layer on the **crease**. Push from the left so the point forms a flap. Flatten the flap to the right.

8

Fold the flap down as shown. Turn the model over from side to side. Repeat steps 5 through 8 on the other side.

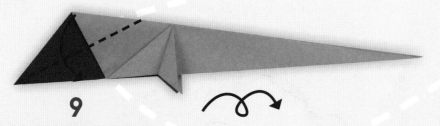

9

Valley fold the top point to the bottom edge. Turn the model over from side to side and repeat on the other side.

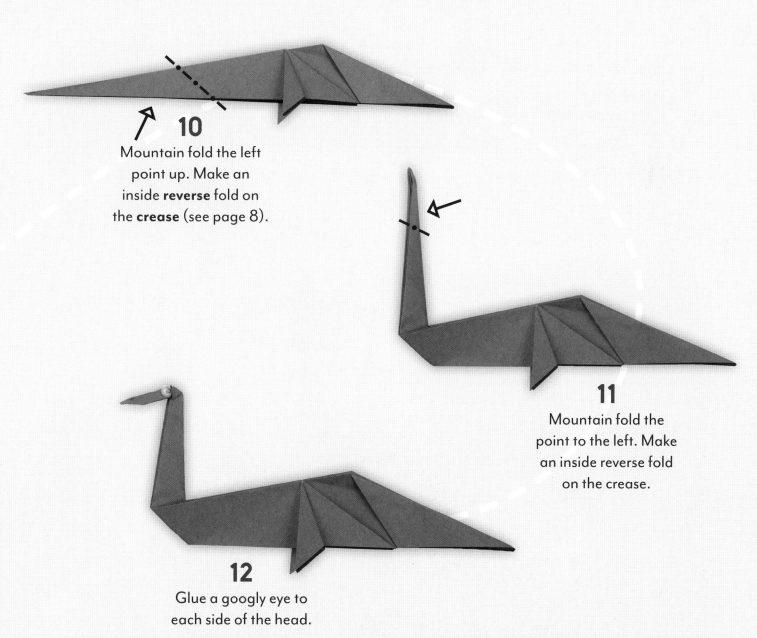

10

Mountain fold the left
point up. Make an
inside **reverse** fold on
the **crease** (see page 8).

11

Mountain fold the
point to the left. Make
an inside reverse fold
on the crease.

12

Glue a googly eye to
each side of the head.

FLYING
PTERANODON

- paper (square)
- googly eyes
- glue

1

Place the paper on the table with a straight edge at the top. Your dinosaur will be the color of the faceup side.

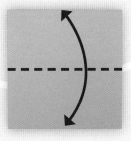

2

Valley fold the bottom to the top. Unfold.

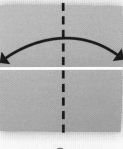

3

Valley fold the right side to the left side. Unfold.

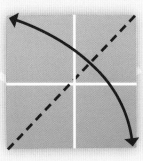

4

Valley fold one point to the opposite point Unfold.

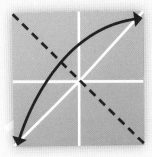

5

Valley fold the
other two points
together. Unfold.

6

Turn the paper
over. Place it
with a straight
edge at the top.

7

Valley fold the
top right point
to the center.
Repeat with the
top left point.

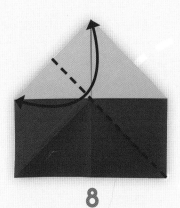

8

Fold the top point to
the left point. Unfold.

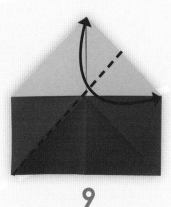

9

Fold the top point
to the right point.
Unfold.

Continued
on the
next page.

29

10

Valley fold the side points to the bottom edge. Flatten the top point over them.

11

Valley fold the side points on the top layer to the center **crease**.

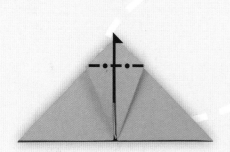

12

Mountain fold the top point. Unfold the last three folds.

13

Lift the top layer of the bottom point. Push the side points together. Flatten the sides. This is similar to step 5 of the bird base. (See page 11.)

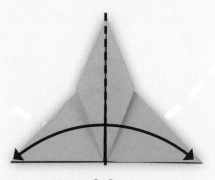

14

Valley fold the right point to the left point. Unfold.

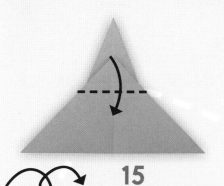

15

Turn the model over from side to side. Valley fold the point on the top layer. The top points are the beak and **crest**.

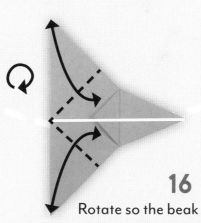

16

Rotate so the beak points to the right. Valley fold the top and bottom points to the center **crease**. Unfold. These are the wings.

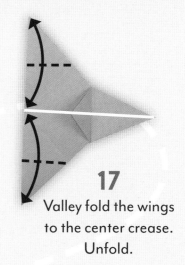

17

Valley fold the wings to the center crease. Unfold.

18

Mountain fold the tips of the wings.

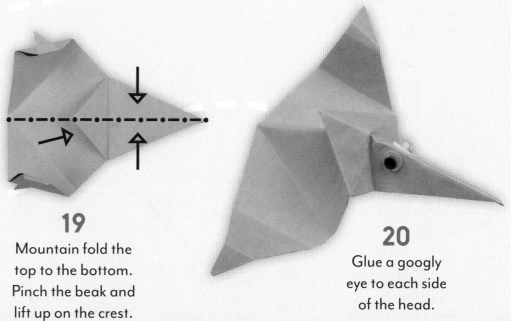

19

Mountain fold the top to the bottom. Pinch the beak and lift up on the crest.

20

Glue a googly eye to each side of the head.

GLOSSARY

accurate — exact or correct.

amaze — to surprise or fill with wonder.

crease — 1. a line made by folding something.
2. to make a sharp line in something by folding it.

crest — a raised area or a tuft of hair or
feathers on an animal's head.

diagram — a drawing that shows how something
works or how parts go together.

optional — something you can choose, but is not required.

outer — on the outside.

reverse — backwards, in the opposite direction.

snout — the jaws and nose of an animal.

symbol — an object or picture that stands for or
represents something.